Animals in the
Mountains

By John Wood

KidHaven
PUBLISHING

Published in 2018 by
KidHaven Publishing, an Imprint of Greenhaven Publishing, LLC
353 3rd Avenue
Suite 255
New York, NY 10010

Designer: Matt Rumbelow
Editor: Holly Duhig

Cataloging-in-Publication Data

Names: Wood, John.
Title: Animals in the mountains / John Wood.
Description: New York : KidHaven Publishing, 2018. | Series: Where animals live | Includes index.
Identifiers: ISBN 9781534523715 (pbk.) | 9781534523692 (library bound) | ISBN 9781534525146 (6 pack) | ISBN 9781534523708 (ebook)
Subjects: LCSH: Mountain animals–Juvenile literature.
Classification: LCC QL113.W66 2018 | DDC 591.74'6–dc23

3 5944 00140 0785

Printed in the United States of America

CPSIA compliance information: Batch #CW18KL: For further information contact Greenhaven Publishing LLC, New York, New York at 1-844-317-7404.

Please visit our website, www.greenhavenpublishing.com. For a free color catalog of all our high-quality books, call toll free 1-844-317-7404 or fax 1-844-317-7405.

Photo credits: Abbreviations: l-left, r-right, b-bottom, t-top, c-center, m-middle.
Covertr – Steve Boice; Covertm – Raimon Santacatalina; Covertl – Tom Reichner; Coverbl – Khoroshunova Olga; Coverbr – Warren Metcalf. 2 – Ruslan Gusev. 3: bg – Chaikom; br – Dudarev Mikhail. 4 – Vitalfoto. 5: tl – badahos; m – leungchopan; bl – dugdax; br – Willyam Bradberry. 6 – Vixit. 7 – celio messias silva. 8 – kavram. 9 – Anton_Ivanov. 10 – Raimon Santacatalina. 11 – Karel Bartik. 12 – dangdumrong. 13 – Khoroshunova Olga. 14 – Warren Metcalf. 15 – Brian Millenbach. 16 – Pavel Svoboda Photography. 17 – Pavel Svoboda Photography. 18 – Steve Boice. 19 – Julie Lubick. 20 – Victor Lauer. 21 – trekandshoot. 22 – Andywak. 23 – Tom Reichner.
Images are courtesy of Shutterstock.com, with thanks to Getty Images, Thinkstock Photo, and iStockphoto.

CONTENTS

Words that look like this can be found in the glossary on page 24.

WHAT IS A HABITAT?

A habitat is a place where an animal lives. It provides the animal with food, shelter, and everything else it needs to survive.

4

There are many different habitats in the world. Each one is home to several different animals.

jungles

mountains

oceans

forests

MOUNTAINS?

Mountains are tall, rocky rises in the Earth. On tall mountains, the summit is usually cold and covered in snow.

Mount Everest is the tallest mountain in the world.

6

When a group of mountains are together in a row, it is called a mountain range. Mountain ranges can be long and some pass through many countries.

The Andes is the Earth's longest on-land mountain range.

MOUNTAIN HABITAT

Mountains are home to many different habitats. Lower down a mountain there can be forests and lakes. This is because it's warmer and there is more rainfall.

mountain forests

8

Higher up a mountain is the tundra. Only tough grass and mountain flowers grow in this habitat because it is too cold for trees.

mountain tundra

The tree line is the point where the trees stop growing.

9

GOLDEN EAGLES

Golden eagles are found in mountains all over the world. They usually make their nests high up in trees or on the side of cliffs.

A golden eagle's wingspan is around 6.5 feet (2 m). That's as wide as a car!

A golden eagle has claws on its feet called talons.

Golden eagles generally hunt rabbits. Sometimes they hunt bigger animals, such as deer. They catch their prey by quickly diving from high in the sky.

11

GIANT PANDAS

Giant pandas live in forests which are high in the mountains of China. They like to live alone and avoid other pandas most of the time.

Giant pandas are good at climbing trees.

A giant panda's diet is mostly made up of a plant called bamboo. Pandas often spend around 12 hours of their day eating.

Pandas eat a lot of bamboo.

COUGARS

Cougars live in the mountains of the United States. Cougars are also called mountain lions, panthers or pumas. These are all different names for the same animal.

Cougars mostly eat deer, but sometimes hunt smaller animals such as foxes and mice. Cougars have strong hind legs which they use to jump a long way.

Cougars also spend most of their time alone.

15

ALPACAS

Alpacas come from the mountains of South America. Although alpacas live in the mountains, they are all owned by humans.

There are no wild alpacas.

a herd of
alpacas
grazing

When a group of alpacas live together,
it is called a herd. They talk to each
other by humming, and spit and
shriek if they feel scared.

MOUNTAIN GOATS

Mountain goats live in North America. They have hooves that are soft in the middle, which make it easier to grip the small, rocky ledges.

mountain goats going down a cliff

Mountain goats mostly eat grass. They live together in herds and stay safe from predators by moving quickly around the steep mountain cliffs.

DANGER

When harmful gases from cars, airplanes and factories are released into the air, they can trap heat in the Earth's atmosphere, making the planet hotter. This is called global warming and it is putting mountain animals in danger.

Global warming can make mountain habitats hotter. This makes it harder for animals to survive. When an animal is finding it hard to survive, it is said to be endangered.

SNOW LEOPARDS

Snow leopards live in the mountain tundra. They are endangered because global warming is causing their habitat to shrink, which means they have less space to find food.

AMERICAN PIKA

The American pika is also endangered. They also like to live in the cold mountain tundra but global warming is making it too hot for them to survive.

GLOSSARY

diet	things that an animal usually eats
endangered	when an animal is in danger of dying out
gas	an air-like substance that moves around freely
graze	when an animal eats grass
hind leg	back leg
predator	an animal that hunts other animals
prey	animals that are hunted by other animals
shelter	protection from danger and harsh weather
summit	highest point of a mountain
tundra	a cold area where trees do not grow
wingspan	the distance between the tip of each wing when stretched out

Index

5/2018

P
Animals
591.746
Woo

19